Dedication

To my family, who gave me my roots.
To my teachers and mentors, who have enabled me to sprout.
To the community that has helped me blossom.
Thank you all for letting me thrive in this forest called Life.

And to every kid who has stood between two worlds, this is for you. My passion for dance has helped me find my place, my courage, my resilience, and my identity.

I hope your passions help you with your self-discovery too.

With all my heart,
Tara

First published in India by HarperVantage, 2025

An imprint of HarperCollins Publishers
HarperCollins Publishers India, Cyber City, Building 10-A, Gurugram,
Haryana-122002, India
www.harpercollins.co.in

2 4 6 8 10 9 7 5 3 1
Copyright © For I am Me, LLC, 2025

P-ISBN: 9789373070575

E-ISBN: 9789373072029

The views and opinions expressed in this book are the author's own and the facts are
as reported by him/her, and the publishers are not in any way liable for the same.

Tara Srinivasan asserts the moral right
to be identified as the author of this work.

All rights reserved. No part of this publication may be reproduced,
stored in a retrieval system, or transmitted, in any form or by any means,
electronic, mechanical, photocopying, recording or otherwise,
without the prior permission of the publishers.

Without limiting the exclusive rights of any author, contributor or the publisher of
this publication, any unauthorized use of this publication to train generative artificial
intelligence (AI) technologies is expressly prohibited. HarperCollins also exercise their
rights under Article 4(3) of the Digital Single Market Directive 2019/790 and expressly
reserve this publication from the text and data-mining exception.

HarperCollins Publishers, Macken House, 39/40 Mayor Street Upper, Dublin 1,
D01 C9W8, Ireland

Printed in India by Replika Press Pvt. Ltd.

FOR I AM ME AND I AM STRONG

by Tara Srinivasan

HARPER VANTAGE

An imprint of HarperCollins Publishers

Once upon a time, deep in the heart of Texas, lived a young, cheerful girl named **TARA.**

Tara had two older brothers that she adored.

Ever since she was a baby, Tara loved to dance. Even though she was the youngest, she would win every single dance competition against her brothers.

Whether the stage was the coffee table or an Indian wedding, she loved to groove to a tune.

Since Tara loved to dance, she started taking a lot of classes. And because her family was from India, she signed up for lessons in Bharatanatyam (ba-ra-tuh-naa-tee-yum).

Tara learned that Bharatanatyam is the oldest Indian classical dance form and began in the temples of Tamil Nadu, a state in southern India.

She also began taking classes in ballet, contemporary, hip-hop, and jazz.

Soon, Tara began to notice something.
She was enjoying jazz and hip-hop a lot more than Bharatanatyam.
She had friends! She loved the costumes!
She heard the songs on the radio!
In her jazz and hip-hop classes, the passion she felt was unlike anything else.

Her Bharatanatyam classes were a different story.

For one, Tara didn't have any friends there. The music sounded really different from anything else she'd ever heard. She didn't understand the complex stories about Indian gods. Even the costumes were kind of uncomfortable.

Bharatanatyam started to feel like something Tara had to do instead of something she wanted to do.

Tara felt stuck. None of her friends from hip-hop or jazz classes could relate to her struggles. They weren't Indian and they didn't know anything about Bharatanatyam.

Meanwhile, her Bharatanatyam classmates were quitting left and right. They wanted to focus only on hip-hop. Soon, Tara started to wonder whether she should quit Bharatanatyam too.

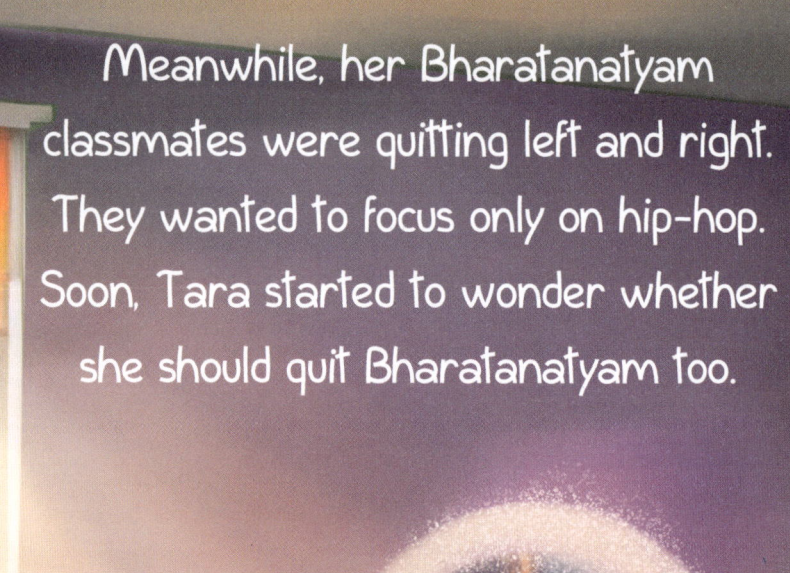

One day, Tara realized something. For every class she walked in cranky, she always walked out smiling. What would happen if she decided to walk into class smiling? She decided to try it.

The more she walked in smiling, the better she got at Bharatanatyam. The better she got, the more she wanted to practice. Before she knew it, she wasn't just improving—she was actually enjoying it.

Tara discovered there were more important things she liked about Bharatanatyam. It became a bridge that connected her to the colorful world of Indian history and culture.

With all the stories of Hindu gods and demons, she could use her imagination and be creative with her expression, style, and emotion.

Her dance movements became more fluid, her expressions more powerful, and her confidence grew on-stage.

Tara could combine the elegance of ballet, the facial expressions of jazz, and the precision of hip-hop with the rhythms of Bharatanatyam dance. Before long, as she made improvements in Bharatanatyam, all of her dance techniques started to improve.

Tara's hard work and resilience began to pay off. After ten years of Bharatanatyam lessons, her teacher told her it was time for her milestone graduation event—her Arangetram (A-rung-gay-trum).

Her Arangetram would be a three-hour solo dance show consisting of eleven dance pieces with a live orchestra and over 350 people in the audience. Her longest piece would run forty-five minutes!

On the day of her Arangetram, she danced through each piece, putting her all into every movement, every breath, and every facial expression. After three long hours, Tara finally finished her very last moves. She could barely stand! Yet, she beamed with pride and joy.

Just then, the audience stood up and cheered for her. Tara couldn't hold back her tears. All her hours, weeks, and years of practice had been so worth it.

Tara felt a new rush of confidence in who she was. From that day on, she knew she was an Indian and an American. A jazz dancer and a Bharatanatyam dancer. She didn't have to choose.

She could hold all the dances she loved inside her, making her style uniquely hers. She was an Indian ballerina and an American Bharatanatyam dancer.

She was not a quitter.
She could do anything.

For she was Tara and she was strong.

About the Author

Tara is a rising high school junior and social entrepreneur who channels her diverse passions toward meaningful impact. She has been a dedicated dancer for over a decade with formal training in both Indian classical and Western dance forms. At fourteen, she completed her Arangetram, a rigorous solo Bharatanatyam dance performance lasting around three hours under the guidance of her guru, Vidhya Mani. Subsequently, she has performed at iconic Indian temples such as Guruvayur and Chidambaram, where she was honored with the title 'Illam Natya Narthagi'. She is also a member of Hyline, the award-winning varsity dance team at Westlake High School.

Tara's passion for dance has sparked numerous initiatives aimed at empowerment and inclusion through dance. Her story of perseverance and cultural diversity is portrayed in Centerstage, a PBS documentary. She also led a lecture-workshop on the role of dance in supporting teen mental health at the 2025 SXSW EDU conference. Tara has taught dance to children through camps with the Andy Roddick Foundation and the Miracle Foundation, including at orphanages in rural India. She also serves as a Kind Leader with The Kindness Campaign.

Beyond the stage, Tara is an avid hiker and one of the youngest individuals to summit Mt. Kilimanjaro (2022) and climb Everest Base Camp (2024). She lives in Austin, Texas, with her family and their Labradoodle, Lotus.

About the Illustrator

Rabindra Nath Barman is a professional illustrator from India, widely recognized for his vibrant and expressive artwork in children's literature. With over a decade of experience in the field, he has illustrated numerous books for young readers, collaborating with publishers and authors both in India and internationally.

Dedicated to storytelling through images, Rabindra believes that illustration is not just about drawing—it's about understanding a child's world.

Rabindra is the founder of ArtoonStation.com where he showcases his portfolio and collaborates on creative projects with authors and publishers worldwide.